We all have an angel
who is always beside us,
who never abandons us
and helps us not to lose our way....
No one journeys alone.

Pope Francis

Under the direction of Romain Lizé, Executive Vice President, Magnificat
Editor, Magnificat: Isabelle Galmiche
Editor, Ignatius: Vivian Dudro
Translator: Janet Chevrier
Proofreader: Claire Gilligan
Assistant to the Editor: Pascale van de Walle
Layout Designers: Élisabeth Hebert, Gauthier Delauné
Production: Thierry Dubus, Sabine Marioni

Printed in June 2018 by Tien Wah Press, Malaysia. Job number MGN 18011
Printed in compliance with the Consumer Protection Safety Act, 2008

WATCH OVER ME

Little
Angel

Text by
Sabine du Mesnil

Illustrations by
Gemma Román

MAGNIFICAT · Ignatius

God loves you so much,
he gave you an angel, an angel he chose
just for you from among all the angels in heaven,
who stand before God and worship him.

From the dawn of time, your angel has awaited you.
When you were only as big as a grain of sand
inside your mommy,
he was watching over you.

Ever since that wonderful day when you were born
your angel has been there, close to you.
He will always be with you!

You are so precious in God's eyes
that he sent an angel to protect you.
Have no fear, for you are safe
in the shelter of your angel's wings.

When you play, your angel guards your steps.
When you are away from home
without Mommy or Daddy, you are not alone.
Your angel is there!
He whispers good things you should do or say.
He helps you in secret!

When you go to Mass, your angel goes with you
and watches over your heart.
Even when you misbehave, he remains with you
and guides you back to the right path.
Your angel is patient with you, just like God!

At night, when you close your eyes and fall asleep,
your angel watches over you
and prays in silence.

Your angel opens up heaven for you.
He carries your prayers up to God
like a bouquet of flowers.
Then he comes back down with an armful of graces:
these are God's gifts to you!
For God knows exactly what your heart needs:
patience, wisdom, courage....

The Bible tells the story of a young man named Jacob.
In a dream, he saw a ladder leading to heaven.
Angels were going up and down it.
Angels travel between heaven and earth;
they are God's messengers!

Do you like the caress of a gentle breeze on your face?
Its freshness does you good even though you can't see it.
You can't see your angel either because angels are invisible.
God, the source of life, created them as pure spirits.
They don't have bodies; they don't eat or sleep.
They don't go to school; they are already full of divine wisdom

Your angel is totally devoted to God:
to loving him, praising him, and serving him.
What joy it is for an angel to obey God!
The love of God gives your guardian angel the wings
to comfort, guide, and encourage you.
Perhaps he has already surprised you,
even saved you from danger!

Your angel shines as brightly as the light of God,
as a reflection of his beauty and goodness.

Your guardian angel is as unique as you.
Everyone has his very own angel:
your mommy, your daddy, your little brother, your friends....

Even those who don't believe in God have a guardian angel!
And those who choose to do bad things have one too!
That's because God loves everyone and desires
to gather all his children close to him.
He never gives up on us.

Your angel wants to lead you
into the great joy of heaven with Jesus!
Every time you listen to your angel,
you taste some of the joy that awaits you.

Your angel has known you since you were very tiny.
He will always care about you.
You can say good morning to your angel,
as you would to a friend.
You can tell your guardian angel about your day,
your joys, and your worries.
You can ask his advice.

When you're sad or afraid, call on your angel!
He will bring you the comfort of God.
If you have bad thoughts, pray to your angel!
He will bring you good thoughts from God.
When you are angry with someone,
ask your guardian angel to speak to his angel.
They will share the peace of God
so that you can share it too.

The angels never stop singing the praises of God:

Gloria, gloria in excelsis Deo!
Glory to God in the highest
and on earth peace to people of goodwill.

You too can often think of God,
to thank him, to praise him,
to sing to him, to listen to his Word.

The more time you spend with God,
the more you become like an angel for others,
bringing them peace and joy,
being a little ray of God's sunshine.

The whole Church celebrates
the Feast of the Guardian Angels on October 2.
Don't forget to give your angel a little wink on that day!

Every day, in the secret of your heart,
you can say this beautiful prayer to your angel:

Angel of God, my guardian dear,
to whom God's love commits me here,
ever this day (or night) be at my side,
to light and guard, to rule and guide.
Amen.